Devotions to my Soul

Teddy Kinget

BookLeaf Publishing

India | USA | UK

DEDICATION

For my ancestors who have passed on and guide me from the beyond.

For Mother Mary, Jesus, Mary Magdalene and all the wild divine saints who inspired and healed.

For the Cailleach for her sturdy support in the storms.

For my brother, who believed me immediately.

For the Teddys, the ancestors, the saint, the self.

A litany of children's cries

The church fills their modern catacombs
With the unmarked bodies of children.
The church tells stories
Of 13 year old Philomena and 12 year old Maria
Gorreti,
Praising their virgin bodies slaughtered
While pissing on the graves of children they
Raped and murdered for sport.
Children's blood seeps into the earth,
Buried under septic tanks,
Tossed into open pits.
The smell of their flesh burns through the air,
Infants in ovens,
Crying out so softly to be saved
from this hell of salvation.

Here Lies Flannery, the Girl who Wasn't

Sometimes I think about the Flannery who
wasn't.
I wonder how soft and gentle her laugh must be.
Or loud and fierce. how it's the right
combination in the right time and place.
I wonder about her first memories,
the ones that weren't panic attacks
or dissociation out of body experiences.
I wonder if they cry when they're angry, or if
they learned how to roar instead.
I wonder what tattoos they put in the places that
don't have scars anymore.

I hope I would like The Flannery that Wasn't.
The Flannery that didn't have to claw her way to
life. The Flannery who had a childhood home in
Safety and Rest.

I like to think she's a painter,
Painting under willow trees, next to river
streams.

Humans walk Among Gods

Your parents are only human,
They say,
Trying to be comforting.
But I have become a god
Through the process of birthing myself
From the ashes of their trauma,
My trauma,
Our trauma.

I see my mother in myself,
As she saw herself in me
When I was a child.
She begs for me to spoon feed her.
To say no feels like starving her,
Another similarity between our mothering
styles.
"You must learn to eat on your own."
I whisper as I clench my hands in my lap.

My father holds silence close to him,
A quiet barrier between him and the world.
"He just won't talk about some things."

What is unknown is unusable.
He has four children,
who needed attention,
who needed praise,
who needed his voice.
He looks out to the mountains.
The house has lost the ring of children's
laughter.

Wild Gardening for The Future

I hope everyday
you do something kind
for yourself and
something kind
for another.
Over and over again,
like planting seeds,
recklessly
optimistic
that every one will grow into a tree.

My body is speckled-
spots on a tree from where her branches have
snapped off
in brutal storms
or passing creatures.
Each spot an eye,
seeing nothing
but retellings.

I hope every day you
recklessly

optimistically
plant kindness like seeds,
Despite knowing
that even trees
suffer the loss of self.
I hope that new sprouts
recklessly
optimistically
root in your skin,
and you become a forest.

Why the Songbird Sings The Morning After Tremendous Sorrow

My joy and laughter rattle down the hallway,
An act of tenacious resistance.
As the monster stood above me to destroy me,
I looked up, and amid my screams and tears,
I laughed,
Deep, hearty, refusing to die laughs.
Like the sunrise and birds,
I met death with joy and resilience.
You cannot silence me
I sang down at her,
You cannot silence me
You cannot silence me
You cannot silence me
For I rise like dandelions on a sweet spring day.

A Prayer of Reclamation

You have a funny sort of love
With your prayers and your hells and your
condescending condemnations said through
sickly sweet condolences.
And you wonder why
Your child, your queer, angry, gay as fuck child,
struggles with her funny sorts of love.
Why can't I just find a nice man? A nice,
catholic, normal man?
Why can't I let the same chains that held me
down and cut into my skin,
Causing neat, straight scars,
Choke me into silence.
Look, no one else has screamed before, you say.
Look, I scream, do you not see their slit throats?

I bring down the old churches with my screams,
And in their place, I build cathedrals for the
dripping cunts, power dykes, flaming faggots.

Behold my creation, I orgasm. May this creation
be a brilliant blasphemy to the cruel hatred of

your church. May your church die as it has
killed every indigenous, queer, Black, heretical
screamer and may this new creation rise like the
flames of Notre Dame.

And so,

We Scream.

Fall Reminders

The geese squawk in the night
Follow us follow us
A moment of jealousy passes through
To flee this winter's silent hopelessness
For warmer skies seems so tempting
But they remind me as their cries fade away
That soon spring will carry their calls back to me
We return we return
They call through the clouds

May 25, 2020

Mary held her dead brown son,
Killed by the state to squash the uprising.
Her tears ran with his blood down his body as
she wailed.
His blood on her face as she held his beaten
body to her chest.

Mama
Mama
I can't
Some water or something
I can't breathe.
Please.
I can't breathe.

I have boiled your rotten flesh from my bones

My bones have been boiled from your rotting
flesh. I am the child of stone and ocean. I stand,
your blood anointing me. You no longer flow
within my veins;

rather you flow over me,
water off a duck's back.

I am sovereign.
My body is my own.
You have no claim to me anymore.

My bones have been boiled and bleached of
your rotting flesh. I have heard your screams of
anger. I have heard your screams of anguish.

My body holds the scars of your abuse. Your
blood anoints me, as the blood of the fallen
enemy anoints the victorious warrior.

I am sovereign.

I stand at the mouth of this cave. Beside me
stands myself, a child, and myself, a crone.

I am you, I whisper as I look into my eyes.

I claim her as my own, the Cailleach proclaims.
Child of stone and ocean. Creation of life and
death.

I leave you in your cave to bury yourself.

I have boiled your rotted flesh from my bones. I
am reborn a child of stone and ocean.

I am sovereign.

The return

She built her alter in my bones,
Rocky crags, rolling hills.
Come home, she cries out to me,
Child of the cailleach.
I wonder far,
My body carrying her earth,
Come home, she calls.
My body holds the graves of grandmothers,
Their stories weaving rope within my muscles,
Come home, she speaks.
I carry her alter in my bones until
I return.
I carry the sacrifices, spilt blood, crushed bone,
stolen bodies, dead children, mothers' cry
Woven like rope around my body.
Come home, she whispers.

I am coming home, I call,
Laying down my burden.

As Notre Dame Burned, Our Lady Wept with Rage

You stood together in a crowd
Holding candles
Praying to Our Lady
For Cardinal Pell.
The tongues of flame
Forced to shine a light in the darkness
he created.

You stood before Her children-
In righteousness indignation
Proclaimed that the cries of
Anger, fear, betrayal and judgement
Aligned us through the Devil's blood
With evil.

You took your holy pen and
Wrote that it was not your priests,
Bishops, cardinals, or responsibility.
But it was homosexuality.
It was the ability to choose.

But - lest we forget -
your priests did not choose.
Satan tempts them too much.

And so we rose as Christ from the dead.
The spirit of the fires,
lit for sympathy of a man who raped boys after
mass,
The spirit of the fires
that burned saints and witches at the stakes,
The spirit of the fires
that raged through the lands you tried to claim,
Rose through the spiral of Notre Dame,
The crackling wood echoed the cries of victims
killed by suicide, addiction, silence.
As the world watched,
Our Lady destroyed.

Scorched earth creates fertile ground

You don't know you're rotting even as your
putrid muscles fall from the bone,
You don't smell the stench of your own
unhappiness,
A puberty of self hate.

The leaves on the trees create a splendor in their
yearly death,
And I think of the flames that destroyed me also
kept me warm.
The irony is that scorched earth encourages the
forest to breathe again.

A symphony for Sappho

You forget how loud silence is after screaming.
I forgot what tenderness meant after
manipulation.
Soft slow touches with soft slow moans stir
within me a tightness in my throat.
I open from the inside out and I feel my world
shift beneath my stirring body.
For the first time in a long time
I tell myself I am safe and I believe it.
I rebuild my foundations, shaky breath by
shaking breath.
I feel my body take root
As I compost my trauma,
Perhaps I will bloom.

Letting go of small traumas

We carry baskets of burdens upon our hips,
The wicker imprinting on our skin.
Generation after Generation
We carry the weighted shadows of the worries of
our mothers.
We collect men who need us, like berries in a
field,
And even if we drop them, their sins stain our
fingers.
And as their juice runs down the lips of others,
We are forced to wash our hands.

The nectar of reclamation

My body is my own. Deliciously,
delightfully,
dangerously,
My Own.
I am drunk with the pleasure and power of such
realizations.

new lungs

i thought rebirthing into myself
would be more like
waking up from a bad dream.

instead,
growing into the human i want to be
is a constant abandonment

of the familiar pain,
the comforting hurt,
the persistent ache.

no one told me that waking up from the dreams
would mean gasping for air
for the first time

and i've never inhaled before.

the saddest eyes

Her eyes are dark, sad, overwhelmed.
this little child, in her striped shirt, holding a
baby,
looks both so small and so old.
I wonder when I disappeared in myself.
I see great-grandmother Bernadette staring from
her eyes.
The corners don't crinkle in joy.
They just stare ahead.

Welcome Teddy

I drove home, listening to music,
when suddenly, or slowly,
all at once, over many years,
I realized Flannery was gone.

Hello, I said to myself,
my nameless, new old self.
Hello, I said back.
I'm Teddy.

And I smiled.
My body felt like home again.

The Ammas

In early Christianity,
There were groups of "women" who would
disappear into the desert,
with their books, their knowledge, their
companions.
Many changed their names, hid their bodies, cut
their hair.
They went from women to men, to genderless
beings.
The caves became their libraries, their homes,
their churches.
When they died, their followers learned their
origins.
Rather than tell their stories, they told the
beginnings only.
To the transformed Ammas in the deserts,
I honor your being,
Please honor mine.
May you guide me as I transform too.